FOR LOVE OF THE MUSE

979-8-218-43301-7: Paperback

979-8-218-43345-1: E-book

979-8-218-43346-8: Audio book

Book Design by Nuno Moreira, NMDESIGN

FOR LOVE OF THE MUSE

David Ellis Rissenberg

TABLE OF CONTENTS

for Deanna

Here, let it finally be said,
that all of these words,
all of the these visions
of beauty and of love

are born of nothing
but the pressure
of your chest
upon mine.

Look, I have called to my lover,

but not only she would come...

- Rainer Maria Rilke

PART ONE

Inscriptions

THE GODDESS SPEAKS TO HER DAUGHTER

Thou, my beautiful one,
full of tears,

how well I know
what it is to be
shelterless under the harsh,
relentless hail of broken dreams,

the way completely lost,
as a cold darkness, consuming space,
leaves nothing left to breathe –

but pressing close thy future
to my vast heart's unimaginable fullness,
and penetrating time with a light
that will one day
take you wholly into its arms,

I say to you:

you may yet
be the flowering of the sacred root,

you may yet
become the joyfully showering grace
of fresh hope upon your own daughters,

you may yet
step out from the paths of dark undergrowth,
and find,
overhead,
swimming in the black void
of a deep, warm ocean sky of summer night,
and shining down,
impossibly,
everywhere,

the constellations of an utterly new life.

"It may be that some little root of the sacred tree still lives. Nourish it then, that it may leaf and bloom and fill with singing birds." – Black Elk

MAY YOU

May you, each pristine evening,
fall into a sweet, mystic dream,
of depth after depth after depth,
cradled, gently, in endlessness;

And each pristine morning,
soar into pure, awakening light –
into an ocean of blue –
luminous, and bright.

May your joys and your vision
be ever-blossoming,
ever-unfolding, ever-renewed,
and refreshed,

Life, beginning,
again, and again,
breath after breath after breath
after breath.

WHOEVER YOU ARE

Whoever you are,
someday, may you feel
how the bright radiance
of your eyes, and hair, and skin

rises like a sun
over the spent night sky
of my body,

flooding it
with the bright, warm colors
of a suddenly ravishing dawn.

It's just in forgetting
the primal magnificence of the womanhood
that rays (unknown to you)
from the hidden divinity
of your body and mind –
ever outwards and towards us –
that you hesitate turning aside that cup

from which you drink
those restless, darkening clouds

of your daily name.

PART TWO

Inception

THE CALL (AN EARLY CHILDHOOD WALK THROUGH BRONX PARK)

A late afternoon
in early October,
alongside the pathway
through the park,
in the darkening greenness
of the gently sloping hills,
astonished, I saw
in the quickly fleeing light,
huge, primeval, blackened boulders
standing embedded in the cool dark grass
like sleepless gods,
and heard them,
as though across vast distances
of space
and time,
silently chanting,
in the language
of another world,
deeply veiled prophecies
which unraveled, spiraling endlessly
upwards into the unknown depths of the sky –

from mystery
to mystery.

And walking further
along the path
into the more deeply wooded hills of the park,
something like surging time
was suddenly pulsing everywhere
in the vibrant, living air,
between the trees and swaying branches,

while from overhead
a serious and innerly exultant music
rushed downwards –
streaming,
without restraint,
through my child's soul.

And so, already,
nature and autumn
had begun to play me.

Already the urgent call
to somehow reflect
back into the swirling void
its surging meaning-storm
rushed downwards upon my senses
and startled heart
from the swiftly moving,
light-shifting,
grey-white clouds.

Yes, unmistakably,
from the swift grey-white clouds
hurrying through the ocean-sky
there flooded down ceaselessly,
deep,
slowly rolling waves
of music-light –

streaming down,
upon me,
from far above.

The wind was rushing,
hurtling everywhere now
above the park benches
(with their aging
green-painted wooden planks,
cased in pale arching frames
of cool grey cement),

when suddenly a flurry of black birds
emerged from nowhere,
and sped skywards all about!
rushing upon the rushing sound
of fallen, fluttering
dry-brown leaves
and trailing behind them
mysterious, dark tone-streams,

filled –
over-brimming –
with gestures that both invited
and warned…

And so, already,
even then,
any other path had become impossible –

for my fate
had lifted me up,
and stolen me,
and was carrying me in her arms,
swiftly,
irretrievably,
away from the world of choice.

WHOSE RISING WORDS

Light, sing me.
Sky, breathe me.
Life, become me.

Transform my seeing
into pure resonance.

But such searching, wondering and doubt –
how can I yet trust such voices,
leading me onto pathways
so painfully beautiful,
and mysteriously crushing?

O I fear that unveiling!

I am afraid the light and laughter
of that world
would leave me anchorless
and lost –

rushing and spiraling me
into its silent beauty.

But then, who writes?

Whose rising words
form prayers
to that vision alone?

I watch from a hill overlooking the scene –
the fisherman catches me with his eyes.

Storm clouds part,
and a single ray of light unveils him –
reflects upon his face
the features of an inner mind –

serenely juggling hunger and hope.

PART THREE

Yearning

A SECRET WISH

Have you ever wished
to climb down, under
the closed petals of a flower?

In that glowing chamber –
so soft, so dark, rustling
among the color shadows –

a secret trembles –

hushed…waiting…

and then a voice –

"Finally, you've come –
complete me"

yearning, she whispers.

YOU WHO REACH OUT IN THOUGHT

You who reach out in thought
to higher worlds
for transcendent being
and the meaning of life –

if you simply put your ear to her chest,
as to a seashell,
and listen,

you'll hear the living waves
of the source
of all the vital, procreative forces

in the entire cosmos.

TRIBAL FUSION

As she dances,
looking at you,
you think your smile is matching hers,
but it's not.

For hers is saying
a thousand things,
while yours is saying
only one.

NOW IS THE TIME

Now is the time
to confess your love –

now, while she's here,
and warm, beside you.

Taste, for even a moment,
that unbearable parting,
and from your bursting heart,
the tears will flow and flow.

Let them fall, freely,
without restraint.

Let them fall,
like a life-giving rain
down upon the sacred earth,

drenching the dark,
soul-thirsting soil

with the meaning
of everything.

UNRAVELING

When you feel her pressing
like heaven against your chest,
finally let your heart unravel –

finally let your love flow, freely,
like the river of life
it is aching to become.

The rest of life is dream-like,
and fleeting:

disappearing into darkness,
like a shower of sparks.

BREATHLESS

Breathless,
as you suddenly sense
the full radiance
of her life force
for the first time –

feeling through her hand
the living electric current
passing between you –
filling your body and mind
with a light that is

fresh,
vital,
renewing,
awakening.

(Now, does it not seem strange
that you had imagined angelic presence
as some kind of myth?)

LOVE'S ARROW

Driven to your knees,

outpouring song and half-blind –

stumbling, ravaged, lost

in a forest dense with impossibility,

desperate to find a way out,

with the shaft of love's arrow

still in your chest –

trembling...

THE FACE OF LONGING

Can I hold the rain in my hand?

Lost in the thunder,
the world fades,
but the hunger
remains.

My hair is dripping.

In the far distance,
I see you climbing
the final hill.

I call out,
but the wind
and roiling mists
carry my voice elsewhere.

Already,
you are memory,
and song.

Already,
yours is the face
of my longing.

HAIKU

Lost in her beauty –

Suddenly her name is gone!

Who is smiling now?

HER LIGHTNING

She has lightning for you –

you've felt it
in her gaze,
and turned away.

But if you could
only stop resisting,
and allow all that force to penetrate –

you would then start to become
everything
you were always meant to be.

THE ENKINDLING

After the last kiss good night,
in the mystic light of dusk,
night already rustling,
cold and close,

along the sidewalk,
lost among tree shadows,
you going your way, I mine,

the music of your beauty
still forcefully surging in my chest,

the memory of your hair and lips,
trembling, still, with soft flames,
through all my senses –

astonished,
how the spell of your open gaze
had kindled places
so deeply hidden inside my body,

that as I looked,
all the things of the world
were now burning,
secretly –
from within –

as though the Muse,
walking, invisibly,
just before me,
and softly smiling,

was gently enkindling
their hidden meanings

with her candle.

AUTUMN

As the long road unfurls,
life flashes by.

And from the heart's center,
from the deep, story-poems of childhood,
from those constantly unfailing seeds,
an image rises…

It is autumn,
with the dark winds
rushing urgently
against the last trembling leaves –

the mystical autumnal air,
(so dense with secrets!),
is teeming innerly
with what is
ripe beyond fullness –

with darkly streaming music
that pleads and reflects,
that rises and falls.

Endings are everywhere –
the fruit is heavy.

Yet strength falls ceaselessly
down from the shadows of the unseen
like huge minor chords
of relentless, godlike love –

down-pouring conscious sonority
from the sky,
to the bedrock –

a song raining with eternity.

And the fruit now falling,
heavy with ripeness,
will sink seeds
deeply into the earth,
to rise again
as thunderous trees:

as massive living symbols
of undefeated will.

PART FOUR

Innocence

HAIKU

First day back at school

A bouquet of wildflowers –

There's her new teacher!

LULLABY

My beautiful girl,
with love-shining eyes,

the day, in all its goldenness,
has unwrapped
its treasures for you:
one by one.

So, rest now, nestled and warm,
in a bed of soft down,
under this night-vast ocean
of shimmering stars.

And, as your eyes begin to close,
those radiant star-sisters will let fall
into the deep well of your heart,
their soft, round,
silvery tones,

like glistening drops
of warm, healing rain.

And taking you up
into infinitely tender arms,
holding you close,
will kiss you,
whispering –

"*From starlight*
were you born,
and into starlight
surely return."

Sleep…

A GOODNIGHT KISS

To Sleeping Beauty came the kiss
that broke the enchantment,
and she awoke.

But with this kiss,
the enchantment
is just beginning.

So, sleep well, and deep,
and may you find
something entirely splendid –

(something magical,
and new),

as you set sail
up, beyond the moon –

up, into the broad, glittering,
star-foaming ocean
of dreams.

A NURSERY LULLABY

Now, upon the roses,
night has fallen.

There, the mother, starlight,
bending down to their bed of earth –

love richly outpouring
from star-glimmering eyes –

with star-glimmering lips
touches to the softly folded petals
of her most beloved children,
a goodnight kiss.

Sleep now, little rose children.

(Dark is the garden. In the moonlight
the shadows of branches are dancing!)

A hushed breeze billows the sail,
and the time has come
to set forth
in your moon-white boat of dreams…

And so,
rocked gently on the sea of night,
in the deep-breathing,
star-foaming waves
of their mother's sky-dark vastness,

there is woven, tenderly, into their flowing sap,
with glowing strands of silken, glittering light,
the secret alchemy, that,
up from the dark, moist earth,

raises the fire-colors
of the dawn.

A LOVE TOO SOON

Only moments ago,
I had been a child,
and you, my friend.

But the light
that suddenly shone towards me from your eyes,
the pain of deep yearning upon your face,
and the tender impulses
of infinitely delicate hands
reaching, invisibly, towards me,

came as mysteries
yet far beyond my bearing,
so that I stood helpless before you –

overtaken by confusion and astonishment –
unable to respond.

Later, when we stood together, silently,
at the wood's edge,
lost in twilight,
watching the evening star on the horizon
as she first shyly glistened out,
our hands almost touched.

Remembering you now,
and the almost impossible purity of love
that blossomed then before my eyes,

in those wondrous, and difficult
last moments of my childhood,

my chest aches with emptiness
for the embrace

that could not yet
come to pass.

LINAH EARTHEN

The earth smiled, remembering her.

Smiled, remembering the young girl
whose hands, with loving warmth
daily bathed in those whispering currents of life
that surged everywhere,
softly through the soil.

And so, sent the favorite among her daughters –
that radiant, star-like spirit called "Ever-Beginning" –
to stream, like nascent light, secretly,
up through the girl's delicately searching fingers,

and into her body and heart.

Then, quietly astonished
and basking in the gentle rivulets of new life
now flowing through her,
her glance, suddenly sweeping skywards
to the vastly embracing blue ocean overhead,

saw downwards entering,
through the golden ambiance
of her love's blossoming etheric body,

a rare brightness,

which wove, in moon-shimmering,
silver-silken threads,
ancient symbols of birth,
and unfolding –

a living tapestry of
mythic animals and climbing plant tendrils,
gleaming, and outspread before her –

revealing, finally,
the possibility of impossibility –

how world-wholeness,
now breathing her completely,
would ceaselessly shower,
like kindness,

invisibly electric seeds
of joy and renewal
wherever she passed.

PART FIVE

Struggle

CRUSHED BY PARTING

You fell like a stone
through the harsh black walls of emptiness –

the dying embers of warmth shooting out
and disappearing into darkness,
like tiny lost meteors…

…and yet,
just as that savage fall
was ripping from your hands
the last fraying strands of life,
of hope,

out of the night-dark void
a palm pressed itself against your chest –

endlessly strong, tender, relentless –
pressing…

And, as her fingers, from raw starlight,
weave into the heart of cold crystal
a gently singing glow of rose,

she breathed you –

parting the mind-ravaging currents
flooding with dark thoughts,
and pouring, like sunlight,
through the sacred dance of your body

a richly songful, golden,
blossoming fullness.

And a life of pure, surging flame,
always crying out, ever-desperately,
ever-pleading,
deeply inside of you for birth,

awakened, suddenly,

and with flashing, beckoning eyes,
hurled the bright-glowing, red-golden
seed-spark of beginning
into your heart,
which then began to smile,
and to sing

with a gentle glow of rose.

URGENCY

Closing your eyes, an unknown voice, rising up from the abyss of your psyche, urgently whispers: "*Now, you must leave.... now!*"

Outside, a storm is rising

the wind picks up, the leaves blash wildly in the trees, the branches break off, hurtling through space, when, without warning, your destiny, truth-starved and held back in silence far too long,

bursts from its hiding place, mercilessly stripping away your masks and armor, finally freeing the unbound lightning of your completely naked soul to crash unstoppably electric through your veins –

and, as the dam of the sky bursts, glorying in the drenching rain,
a savage, triumphant laughter breaks from your voice,
thundering up to the ravaging clouds,

as with godlike force you feel the chains of your old life
snapping off –

one by one...

now, who can stop you?

THE ALCHEMIST'S SECRET

Drink now, my love,
the joy of will transformation.

Glistening with savage hope,
these rarefied golden drops,
like the tears of stars,
have the power to wholly transmute
a seemingly impossible emptiness
into a wind-soaring,
black and golden bird

that will crash, again,
upwards from its ashes
like unchained lightning,

into a fierce soul-storm
of far-seeing, vastly reborn,
unbreakably pure triumph –

so that, from the heights,
with the eyes of a sky being
finally returned home,

you may gaze down,
with strength and serenity,
upon the past, present, and future –

freed from happenstance,
to face whatever approaches you

with a fresh,
vitally alive,
towering self-sovereignty.

OCEAN

…her life had come to this…
it was not a dream…

lightning, flashing,
the soul-pounding,
booming thunder of the dark sea,
and of the heavy cloud-shadow-riven down-pouring sky,
the terrifying hollow muffled sound
of breaking, cracking boards,
the boat's hull, finally splintering,
destroyed and collapsing –

and the ocean took her –

took her savagely, and mercilessly,
under into its massively overturning,
surging foam of mountainous,
brutally crashing waves.

Over and over, she rose and fell –
over and over, she was hurtled about
in the dark, raging foam,
under the freezing,
dark, sky-crashing rain…

…yet, then,
even while desperate, and drowning,
even while submerged, exhausted,
and finally beaten by that vast, roiling intensity –

a fierce, screaming passion of survival
suddenly crashed like primal will
through her soul and through her body –

outstripping in force all the pounding,
riotous demonic elements of the sea –

as if a galactic spear of spirit-lightning,
of towering, goddess-like strength,
had been hurled to explode
deep within the core of her being.

And there,
displacing every atom of her old life,
a kindred galactic force,
a roaring, primeval, commanding force
rose up, igniting, and transforming her soul.

And there,
the immense, alien world of ocean,
with all its dark power, depth and staggering weight,
became her home,
became her kingdom,
became her savage dance.

Its massive force and strength
became the gestures of her arms,
became the gestures of her heart,
of her vision.

And she gloried there in her new being,
spilling forth bright laughter like a goddess
into those deep, echoing caverns of eternity,

as the strange certainty –
that this had always been her homeland –
rose quietly within her,

bathing her,
rainbow-like,
in all the rich, warm colors of life,

like a summer dawn.

PART SIX

Healing

All that heaviness
was imaginary

now

fly

AS WHEN SOFT FINGERS

As when soft fingers
so lightly press against your lips,

as when hands
quietly rest upon your shoulder,
or so gently press against your chest,

the warm, life-giving current flows –

awakening,
encouraging,
healing –

so I touch you now.

AN INVISIBLE KISS

At times her emptiness is crushing.

Passing her in the street,
or catching her glance
across a crowded café –

it hurts,
as you feel the dark,
helpless weight she carries
falling through your body.

Kiss her,
unknowingly, then,
and watch
as, gently startled,

her eyes slowly widen and smile.

As if a butterfly,
suddenly appearing in the afternoon's
warm, golden haze,

brushed ever so lightly,
against the cool,
living softness of her cheek,

those impossibly bright colors

of weightless,
fluttering
joy.

WAITING

Weren't you always waiting

for something

to gently and lovingly lift you above

all the noise and confusion

so that you could bathe weightless

and free and smiling and whole

in the golden sunlight

of childhood once again?

CRADLING

Cradling

your body

in warmth

pressing

so closely

like heaven

REST

Rest, my friend,
my love.

Rest, quietly now,
here, in my arms.

Let time,
with all its maddened events,
hurtle by elsewhere –
distant,
softened.

Allow yourself,
at last,
the wondrous joy of that pure,
deep,
falling…

THOSE WELLING TEARS

Those welling tears...

with this kiss –

a storm of hope.

THE TENDEREST KISS

The tenderest kiss –
lips with infinite warmth
serenely pressing yours.

And suddenly amazed
that your life
had such a beautifully simple answer,
a smile of radiant innocence
rises from your heart.

And those streams of light,
surging, like laughter,
everywhere through your body,
have a color

that cannot be named.

PART SEVEN

Awakening

LIGHT BREATHING

Gently, breathe light into your mind –

smiling,

because it's so beautiful,

because it's so pure –

sweet,

and freeing.

Soon,

when only light

fills all the inner spaces

where heavy thought clouds used to drift,

what clear, bright expanses

will open inside you!

BLUE LIGHT

What if you were filled entirely
with vast expanses
of brilliant, blue light?

What if you inhaled
this bright, radiant,
blue spaciousness,

so that it filled
your arms legs fingers toes face chest eyes –
until you were *overflowing*

with streaming blue light?

Laughing,
because this lightness
is so freeing,
so exhilarating!

Within you, nothing
but light.

Consent
to this beautiful feeling,
this perfect transparency –

leaving for now
who you were,

and becoming only sky.

MEDITATION

After breathing light for ten seconds,

gently relax the borders of your being –

sensing infinity,

as it rushes in ...

AN UNDISCOVERED MIRACLE

Become transparent.

Simply allow the light to pass through the body and mind,
so that they're filled only with outer-ness.

Always close at hand,
effortlessly and joyfully bringing a sense of freedom
that is borderless –

timeless…

And now,

silence.

DARING THE IMPOSSIBLE

Marshaling your love of life
and all your daring,

invite the living sun itself,
everywhere out-raying
cosmic grandeur and power,

into the tiny, sacred temple
of your body.

PART EIGHT

Soaring

SOARING

Just soar
and smile
taking flight
now and forever

That deep blue of the upper air as you enter it
is limitless
bursting
with brightness, freshness
and freedom

You're returning home
finally

so smile
and soar

FLIGHT INTO THE UNIMAGINABLE

The nascent magic
of your beauty,
and of your love,
can blossom, lushly,

can unfold,
at any moment,
like color into the unimaginable.

Can soar,
on richly unfolding,
richly outspreading
glorious white-golden wings,

into that vastly opening ocean-sky
of your birthright.

AMAZEMENT

Find things that amaze you

one after another

don't give up

A new way of seeing

is everywhere

within your grasp

even now

life becomes poetry

Today

out of love

give yourself

the miracle of childhood

again and again

A STORM OF LAUGHTER

Laughing,

as you hear, again,

that deep, echoing roar –

as you step, refreshed, and elated,

into the foaming whitewater

that rushes madly,

like joy,

through the depths of those primal,

life-thundering canyons

of your heart.

Laughing,

as you welcome,

with opening hands,

that life-giving, soul-drenching

teeming downpour

of wonderment –

of renewal –

of rebirth.

DREAM DIVING

The gorgeous sensation

of slowly falling

freedom

has never been more

delicious

nor space so lush

so green

and golden

till finally

ahhhhh…

the water!

PART NINE

Transformation

MUSING

Far into the night,
alone,
she wandered the dark pathways
leading though the wood,

leaving behind her
all that was familiar,
to muse on those filaments –

those invisibly interweaving
prismatic gleaming threads
that bind each thing

to the single, primal center.

Moonlight,
translucent, delicate, ethereal,
lacing through the leaves,
fell everywhere,

fell upon a beautiful, warm hand,
that wonderingly
she placed upon the bark,
feeling, through the pine's rising vastness,

the heartbeat of the world.

Ah, yes,
there it was,
unmistakably –

a single,
living,
beating,
pulse.

And then,
love itself flowed –
coursing through startled,
deeply awakened fingers,

through the dense bark,
into the heart of the tree,
and outwards

into everything.

THROUGH YOU

My love,
if you simply extend your arm,
slowly, and dance-like,

your beautiful hands and fingers
will ray,
out of themselves,
invisible currents
of love and healing –

warm, golden,
of subtlest electricity –
whether there is a receiver
or not.

For the goddess
streams her forces
ceaselessly through you.

It is through you
she knows and shapes
the outer world.

ORIGIN

Maybe you are so drawn to the ocean
because it is there that you feel,
as by some sky-resonating, cosmic kinship,
how deeply birth-giving is your nature –
your essence –

that what you bring forth,
from the unspeakably miraculous vessel
of your woman's body,
is not only the child –

but that, mysteriously,

from the warm, etheric life substances
that rise and blossom and radiate –
ever out-spiraling invisibly
from your body and eyes and heart and being –

there arises,
as if by grace,

what is most profoundly,
most ravishingly,
and most beautifully poetic,

everywhere –
in everything.

THE BEDROCK

Surrender and fall –
to the center,

like a god,
like a goddess –

dare
to leave your life.

Fall, and fall,
until, at last, there is beneath you
the bedrock –

the foundation of the world,
of all worlds –

the primal solidity
upon which
the dark-seething-ocean-storm of archetypal strength
has mounted the cosmos –

the birthplace of eternity –
the birthplace
of the known,
of the unknown.

Feel,
beneath you,
that ultimate center,

out of which
the infinite universes radiate,
ever-out-spiraling –

the center
to which they cohere,

and, to which,
ultimately,

they return.

THE SUN-FLASHING SWORD

One day you heard,
as wind rushing through leaves,
the voice of your spirit,
calling to you.

It called you back
to that long-forgotten place in your heart
where childhood dreams
lavishly unfold their tales of magic,
and of wonderment.

And you remembered
the story of the hero with far-seeing eyes,
with a sword that flashed in the sun,
and a destiny to be fulfilled, at any cost,

and who now, suddenly awakened,
turned to face you, beckoning,

and laughing
with a towering,
savagely joyous,
savagely unconquerable
certainty.

WHEN THE GODDESS

When the goddess deigns

to dance you

smile

and forget

everything

WHEN YOU FINALLY TAKE THE TIME

When you finally take the time, my love,

to quietly and fully ease your body down

into this warm ocean of existence,

you will feel how the light in your eyes,

and the electric beauty

streaming everywhere forth from you,

is lighting up everything inside me at once,

like the life-giving force

of a new sun.

YOUR ELECTRIC DANCE

That the spell of your dance,
as it sways and throbs
with the radiant, electric beauty
of your hair and face and body

could, like nascent lightning,
pour itself into the body of a man
in such a way
that there arises within him

not only that urgent,
swelling pressure to procreate,

but, invisibly,
streaming into and through his blood and heart
that pulsing, seed-like liquid fire,
resonating, mystically,
with the vital, world-enveloping creative forces –

with those creative forces that ceaselessly
pour themselves out as myth and mystery and truth
into the turning seasons, into the forests and the winds and the rains,

and into the cosmos itself
as it spirals endlessly outwards into fathomless distances –

that the spell of your electric dance,
love-outpouring,
could allow him to merge –

blending and interweaving with these forces –

such that there gushes forth from his throat and voice and hands
living tone,
living images, as song and verse,

is the miracle,
is the grace of the muse that rushes through you
from the primal feminine hurricane of the unknown –

from that starlight-teeming ocean of birth and being
from which there originates everything that exists,

and everything that has yet come to pass.

COOPER LAKE

No longer anyone's voice;

rather, what crept into the blood –

the voice of the goddess.

Through darkly burning vines
entering,

her voice like liquid fire
breathed me,

shook the core,
snapped the chains.

And a dark bird of longing
broke free from my throat
with a piercing cry of release,

saturating the huge night sky
with a pulsating electric freedom –

shattering,

utterly,
and finally,

the dream of containment.

PART TEN

The Embrace

THE TOUCH OF YOUR SKIN

the touch of your skin,
like summer –

plunging into the cool lushness
of your deep, sparkling waters –

a smile bursting like sunlight
through my entire body –

riding like laughter
ocean waves crashing

with timelessness –

with discovery…

THE POET PLEADS WITH HIS MUSE TO TEACH HIM OF LOVE

O thou shining one!
O thou majestic singer of my life's song!

Teach me what dreams are woven
from those currents of love secretly threading
through the living shadows that rise and fall
in thy deep, mysterious, silver night!

With her eyes, far-seeing,
and glistening with the light of distant stars,
she smiles at him, assenting.

And flowing through a woman's form
of such softly, shining beauty –

now, wholly unveiled, warm,
and shimmering with a profoundly sensitive
feminine knowing –

her spirit surges,
with life beyond life.

With love and unbinding,
she touches him
and rushes like awakening,
almost visibly,

through the throbbing atmosphere of his becoming,
through the throbbing color-dreams of his senses,
through those wholly unnamable intimate spaces
of their interweaving, etheric breathing –

healing, inspiring, soothing, caressing,

she tenderly and patiently unravels the subtle,
human knots of his restraint,

such that all the delicate,
innerly light-surging electric fibers
of his bodily radiance crest, wave-like,
surging,

moving out beyond the threshold of sensation,
laughing and spinning and spiraling
through undulant currents of tone,
through vividly turning currents
of liquid, pulsating delight…

until, finally, tenderly interwoven,
and over-brimming with flowering, electric spirit,

she sets them adrift,
and they are lost –

lost, in a silent storm of ravishment.

Utterly, blissfully, lost,
on a shoreless sea,

together, ever-unraveling
the intricate, mystically flowing
harmonies of meaning –

ever amazed,
ever there unwrapping

miraculous gift,
after gift,
after gift.

THE FIERCE CURRENT OF ELECTRIC LOVE

Whatever happens,
stay vividly here -
in this lightning-flash of *nowness*.

Deeply inhaling it,
pressing it to your heart –

second by second.

This is the fiercely,
vitally real,
ever-unflagging,
sparking current
of electric love.

This is existence –

being.

THE EMBRACE

Ah, my love,
I am holding you now in my arms –

but do you know what it is
that is flowing through this embrace?

Hour upon hour of love-infused
golden summer sunlight,

and a surging ocean of music,
with its storms and heaving waves,
and dark air teeming
with those time-opening chasms
of sea spray scent.

(And even,
sometimes,
below the surface,
secret, fathomless depths
of infinite peace.)

Flowing through this embrace
is a lifetime overflowing its brim
with ceaseless searching,

ceaseless discovering,
ceaseless failure,
ceaseless hope.

Flowing through this embrace
is the source of words,
and the destination of words –

words that are yet unborn,
and words that,
having found their way
through the tangled pathways
of a lifetime's bafflingly unwinding intentions,

burst finally through the ether of silence

and emerge,
silent themselves,
once again,
as stars.

Stars strung like letter-pearls
through those sky symbols of night –

through those undiscoverable,
unnamable constellations,
that mystically weave into the loving heart –

that weave with silvery gleaming points
of conscious celestial light
into the cosmic mirror that glows and pulses
in the central core of our being,

meanings far too rich
for words to enfold.

For words, my love,
become as lost in the immensity of that embrace

(of this embrace)

as tiny meteorites,
which, flung far,
far out beyond their depth,
disappear into the star-seething,
night-dark sea.

That disappear into the dark ocean of living warmth

of the arms

enfolding you

now.

THE SECRET OF A MIDSUMMER NIGHT'S OCEAN

Jumping from surf-sprayed rocks
into a darkly star-shimmering,
ravishing ocean of intimacy,

smiling and wide-eyed we plunge,
abandoning ourselves happily
into the arms of its strong currents
and breathing each other's body completely –

our lips finding everywhere the secret, pulsing responses of delight,
our fingers madly entwining, loosening, searching, discovering,
our bodies wholly opening to the life-giving,
awakening rivers of prismatic color,
surging through us and about us –

vastly opening –

our bodies and souls
bursting with light.

While above us,
deeply breathing the summer-warm, night-dark sky,

richly glimmering waves of starry infinitude
roll and crest and break and foam –

crashing blissfully over each other,
like a storm
that secretly teems with revelation.

And we, too, ocean-like, crest and fall:

rising up into star-radiant wakefulness,
submerging into deep watery canyons
that rhythmically gather and outpour –

lifting, plunging, plunging, lifting,

ebbing and flowing with such dance-like grace
that these two worlds
suddenly collapse into a single soaring body of water-light
that, lifting finally beyond fullness,
blossoms into a such a release
that the world of space falls, swooning,

back into itself.

Inhaling deeply, and then,
transformed and renewed,
exhaling –

filling the richly warm expanses of midnight summer air
with the sweetly mysterious fragrance of wild meadow flowers,

and wrapping us, tenderly, at least,

in a silent, restful,
enfolding darkness.

And it is here, my love,
with all our senses interweaving, harmonized,
and radiating purely outwards in all directions
like moonlight –

bathed in bright wakefulness and
embracing world wholeness –

that in pure childlike wonderment

we find ourselves
at the very heart of non-dual being,
in all its cosmic grandeur and splendor –

our chests pressed tightly together
and with fathomless smiles…

falling, falling, falling –

drifting, down, slowly,

into ethereal windswept star-snow –

into a spaceless, timeless, borderless
midsummer night's ocean

of unspeakable love.

TANTRA

Within the dark, voluptuous fire
of love's rapturously unfolding dance –

subtly finding its way within
through the softly caressing flames
of loving hands –

a thought-sensation of incredibly rare brightness
suddenly overtook my senses –

the fact of her being, her identity –

her being alive and here,

her reality,
the simple miracle of her existence,

of who she was –

all of this at once
surged mercilessly through me
like conscious lightning –

magnifying the beauty and meaning
of her fiercely alive body and mind
a thousandfold.

Her eyes flashed that she had understood
exactly what happened,
and with unhesitatingly passionate grace,
entered into it instantly and profoundly.

And so it happened that,
in seeing with such sudden electric certainty
that our warm and gloriously interweaving bodies
were spun entirely with spirit-being

constantly and achingly in search of its origin,

our sense of existence,
of the radiantly pure,
simple reality of being

exploded infinitely –

arcing,
in a single instant
from the shores of the conceivable
to the furthest reaches
of the vast ocean of the inconceivable –

the hugely opening sky of our love
embracing everything,
everywhere…

And there,
in that newly discovered world,

refreshed and reborn,
radiantly alive and awake,

we bathed, quietly,
in the down-streaming,
golden light of a sun

to which our sun

is barely a grain of sand.

THE DARK, LIVING HURRICANE OF YOUR BEAUTY

Naked, unprotected, lost,

in the dark, living hurricane
of your beauty,

music crashes through me –

crashes through my body,
through my voice –

River-rushing
dream-energy
pouring through my veins

life beyond life:
a fierce storm of surrender.

DARING THE THRESHOLD

Though, as you innerly murmur these words,
I can feel the rising, pulsing forces of your soul,
as they spiral out into the night,

(ever unravelling mystically into darkness)

while hungrily and gratefully inhaling
the secret fragrance of their gorgeous colors –

only after having dared the threshold,
and meeting in that astonishing
and unknown life

that breathes and blossoms
beyond the memory of our earthly names,
where we finally can laugh
and bathe together, like children

in the brightly roaring music-ocean
of naked love –

only then
can the delicate, searching tendrils
of our thoughts and feelings

lose themselves and merge
in a dance so wild, so untamable,

so unspeakably free and weightless,
and beneath such a blissful,
softly drenching storm
of soul-ravishing beauty,

that, wondrously,
makes those building, cresting,
and exploding waves of physical union

now seem like the distant,
affectionately half-forgotten dream

of some preparatory life.

IT BEGINS AS A GENTLE PULSING IN THE HEART

It begins as a gentle pulsing in the heart –
quietly my love – just wait..
and listen…

Closing your eyes,
your body slowly fills with its meaning,

and into the vital core of your being
rivers of warmth flow,
finding their way
through undiscovered caverns,
which open now
mysteriously, everywhere,
deep within your body.

Your lips soften,
your chest begins to throb and ache,
as whispers of what is soon to come,
like secrets unraveling against your will,
come flooding through the warmth of your arms,

which, as they reach out in painful yearning,
an embrace of unimaginable fullness
presses itself like heaven against your entire body,
enwrapping you, enfolding you,

as deeply through your center
a sun rises, pulses,
builds and builds in force,
taking you, overtaking you, laughing,

and breaking the last threads of resistance,
suddenly rockets skywards,
piercing the zenith,
bursting!

As the perfect joy
of perfect completeness,
brightly down-flooding through all your senses,

fills the entirely reborn world
now surrounding you

with vivid, awakening light.

BEYOND ALL FAIRYTALE TREASURES

Beyond all fairytale treasures,
beyond the gold and rainbows,
beyond enchantments,

and all the wishes
that magical creatures
could possibly grant –

in each other's arms,
these quiet tears of love.

PART ELEVEN

The Archetype

E V E

When her eyes and smile
flash at us,
our souls overflow
like sunlight, sparkling
from a fountain –

instantly we awaken
into pure existence

with widening eyes,

like song gushing
from the throats of birds
into the bright, morning air.

And when she turns
and looks, musing,
into herself,

we begin to hear,
for the first time,
the true names of things

flowering into words,

as they are born.
within her heart.

WHO SHE IS

Through doorway after doorway,
one approaches you.

But only much later,
only after crossing the final threshold,
and finding within the cave-like,
innermost chamber –

upon an ancient throne of bedrock,
swarming with a lacework
of intricately graven living symbols
that out-spiral invisibly,

that unravel and cast down
to the bottom of the soul's well
the tonal mysteries of origin –

earth's most secret
dreams and desires.

In a ring of dark fire,
flashing,
slowly,

earth-core rumbling up
from the endless depths beneath you –

a distant relentless thunder
of rage and strength
that rises up through the trembling stone,
and into your blood –

as the windstorm of your love
crashes down from the peaks
of the three sacred mountains

and rises up again,
gale-like and turbulent
in your flashing eyes –

only there does one hear,
silently,
as if spoken only to inner ears,

only to the heart yearning secretly
and desperately
amidst the noise of life
for the full weight of truth,

your true name.

WINTER SOLSTICE

From this dark ocean
of falling night,

from she who is
quietly, consciously, ceaselessly,

breathing the sky,
breathing the world,

from she who gave birth
to light itself,

from the outflowing
tenderness of her vast embrace –

kisses of starlight,
for you –

kisses of moonlight,
for you.

AFTERWORD

The Alchemy of Love

THE ALCHEMY OF LOVE

The warm, ocean-atmosphere of life and grace that we live within is alive – it has voice – and if we can stop for a moment, and listen closely, we will hear it, saying:

"Ah, my beautiful darling, dearest child of the miraculously unfolding powers of world love and world intelligence. Open, finally. Open to me, now. For here – suspended between light and darkness – we face that moment.

Feel how I am yearning to breathe you, to dance you, to sing you, to sing your life – to sing it outwards and upwards, filling the fields, the forests, the turning, unwinding seasons, filling the skies.

Feel how I am yearning to enter you, to merge with you, to at last and finally dissolve this strange dream of separateness that once fell upon you unawares, like hypnotic sleep. To enter, streaming like living light, into your being and blood, to finally breathe your life out into that perfect fullness for which it was always destined, from the earliest beginning."

If you wish to sacrifice something in the hope of bringing warmth and beauty and light and joy into the world, sacrifice withholding – sacrifice insularity.

Real magic happens not from what we invent or contrive, however skillfully, but from what we allow the cosmically archetypal and earthly archetypal forces to breathe through us.

Love means turning our will around 180 degrees – to use it not to express what originates from the tiny, enclosed sphere of our personal world, but rather to measurelessly open our being and bodies to the ocean of life, of beauty, of color, of meaning, of birth and renewal.

Then, something will inevitably ray forth from us that the world will feel – responding with grateful tears and with invisible embraces, that will, in turn, radiate back towards us from all directions.

This is the alchemy of love.

ABOUT THE AUTHOR

David Ellis Rissenberg is a poet, musician, husband, and father whose artistic work is dedicated to inspiring in his readers and listeners the conviction that the world of deepest beauty and meaning is, in fact, always close at hand, existing alongside our day-to-day lives, and simply waiting to be recognized and lived into. His debut collection of poetry, *For Love of the Muse*, describes the manifold ways in which the divine spirit of the Muse flows through the world, and the tremendous possibilities for creativity, love, healing, and transformation that can stream through the body and psyche of every woman as the living reality of these forces blossom into awareness.

He and his wife, Deanna, currently live and work from their home, Bramble Hill, in the Catskill Mountains of upstate New York. There he spends his time in his studio, writing poetry, composing, recording, and giving recitals of classical and improvised music on his newly rebuilt 1895 Steinway Concert Grand piano, christened "Celestia".

He would be delighted to have you join him on this ever-unfolding adventure by visiting davidellisrissenberg.com.

Made in the USA
Middletown, DE
16 June 2024

55910171R00096